# Preface

D0513223

This interesting and well-written book provides an excellent insight into the 18th century military roads of Perthshire. The background and context to General Wade's appointment as Commander-in-Chief, North Britain in 1724 are explained, as well as the purpose behind the routes themselves - connecting a network of hastily positioned forts as the government's symbolic eyes and ears in hostile country. The arduous practicalities of constructing Wade's roads and bridges by teams of soldiers are described and illustrated. Ironically, by the time the roads were actively used in the '45, Wade had left Scotland, and for a brief time his roads were arguably of greater benefit to the Jacobite forces. Nevertheless, following the eventual defeat of the Jacobites at Culloden in April 1746, Wade's protégée and successor William Caulfeild oversaw a massive expansion of road building, improving and extending the initial network laid down by Wade.

The book also highlights the importance of maps in understanding Wade's roads. General Wade was a key figure in the Hanoverian conquest of the Highlands, and from a cartographic perspective, he promoted distinctive new military maps of roads, forts and towns. The thinking behind these maps, with their frequent inclusion of Roman roads and forts, and their depiction of the location of hostile clan forces, is also quite revealing. The book nicely illustrates that historic maps have an important role to play in understanding these military roads, and that their value is enhanced by interpreting them with other written evidence. Carefully selected primary sources provide an insight into how the military roads were seen by the engineers and soldiers who actually planned them. Through the success of the military roads in their pacification of the Highlands, both the roads themselves and the mapping of them from the later 18th century were fundamentally different.

Well-referenced, well-researched, and packed with interesting new material, this accessible and informative book is enjoyable to read and helps us to understand and appreciate Wade's military roads today.

Chris Fleet

Chris Fleet
National Library of Scotland

# Scotland's military roads and strongholds

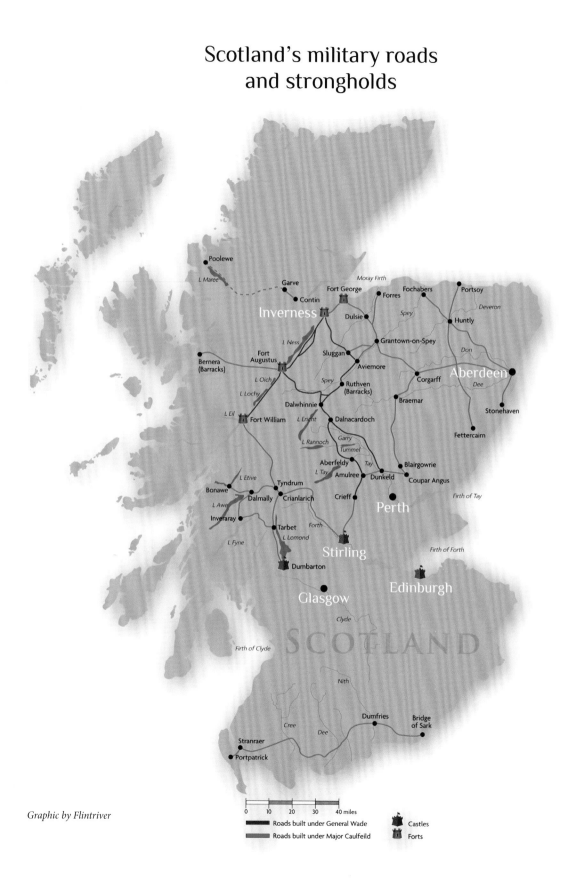

Graphic by Flintriver

Poolewe
L Maree
Garve
Contin
Fort George
Forres
Fochabers
Portsoy
Moray Firth
Deveron
Inverness
Dulsie
Spey
Huntly
L Ness
Sluggan
Grantown-on-Spey
Don
Fort Augustus
Aviemore
Aberdeen
Bernera (Barracks)
L Oich
Spey
Ruthven (Barracks)
Corgarff
Dee
L Lochy
Dalwhinnie
Braemar
L Eil
Fort William
L Ericht
Dalnacardoch
Stonehaven
L Rannoch
Garry
Fettercairn
Tummel
Aberfeldy
Tay
Blairgowrie
L Tay
Amulree
Dunkeld
Coupar Angus
L Etive
Tyndrum
Crieff
Firth of Tay
Bonawe
Dalmally
Crianlarich
Perth
L Awe
Inveraray
Tarbet
Forth
L Fyne
L Lomond
Stirling
Firth of Forth
Dumbarton
Edinburgh
Glasgow
Clyde
SCOTLAND
Firth of Clyde
Nith
Dumfries
Bridge of Sark
Cree
Dee
Stranraer
Portpatrick

0   10   20   30   40 miles

Roads built under General Wade
Roads built under Major Caulfeild
Castles
Forts

# General Wade's Legacy

## The 18th century military road system in Perthshire

### Lindsay Farquharson
### Perth and Kinross Heritage Trust

Published by Perth and Kinross heritage Trust
All images and text are copyright except where indicated
© Perth and Kinross Heritage Trust 2011

Printed and bound by Farquhar and Son Ltd Perth

ISBN 978-0-9564427-6-5

*Front Cover: Field Marshal George Wade attributed to Johan van Deist (Scottish National Portrait Gallery).*
*Back Cover: Map of Scotland showing the forts at Inverness, Fort Augustus, Fort William and Moidart and on which is pencilled*
*the proposed military roads, also the names and numbers of men that could be raised by the various clans by General Wade c. 1724*
*(Reproduced by kind permission of the Trustees of the National Library of Scotland)*

*Perth fortified by the Jacobites during the 1715 Rising*

4

# Revolt and Rising

*The Highlands of Scotland, being a country very mountainous and almost inaccessible to any but the inhabitants thereof, whose language and dress are entirely different … do remain to this day much less civilised than other parts of Scotland, from whence many inconveniences arise…even to the Government itself.*
- from Lord Lovat's address to His Majesty George I, 1724

## Jacobitism is born

In 1725, General Wade initiated a massive overhaul of the military infrastructure in Scotland by constructing and strengthening forts and barracks and connecting them with a network of roads across the Highlands. It was an ambitious and expensive undertaking designed to impose Hanoverian control on a population, many of who were dissatisfied with the ruling regime and who had therefore allied themselves with the Jacobite cause.

Jacobitism as a political cause was born out of the aftermath of the Glorious Revolution of 1688-1689 when William III of Orange overthrew James VII of Scotland (James II of England). In England this episode was so called as it was a relatively peaceful affair but in Scotland and Ireland it was not as straightforward. A Convention of Estates was called in Edinburgh in March 1689 and the following month it had voted almost unanimously to offer the Scottish crown to William and Mary, James' Protestant daughter. A Claim of Right was drawn up that stated that as a professed papist James had forfeited his right to the crown and that no papist could again be king, queen or officer of state in Scotland. The Act also demanded the abolition of Episcopacy. The vote reflected the dominant Whiggish and Presbyterian nature of the Convention as most of James' supporters had left by early March in the face of well-organised opposition and sought to fight their cause elsewhere. John Graham of Claverhouse, Viscount Dundee raised an opposition force predominantly from the Episcopalian and Catholic clans of the Highlands and, along with the Anglican non-jurors, it was these congregations who were to remain the foundation of Jacobitism for the next 60 years. The Jacobite force met the government army at Killiekrankie on 27th July 1689 where they scored an unexpected victory but lost their leader, Dundee, in the final stages of the battle. His death was a major factor in the eventual collapse of the rebellion and by June 1691, the Jacobites finally sent requests to James for permission to surrender to William's rule.

## The 1715 Rising and the capture of Perth

There were further attempted Jacobite risings in 1708 and 1719 with the best chance of success in 1715. The 1707 Act of Union had not been popular with many of the Scottish population and disillusionment increased over the next eight years due to a series of breaches of the Treaty by the British government and delays in honouring financial inducements. The result was that by the time of Hanoverian succession many Scots were strongly considering the possibility of restoring the Stuarts to the throne. Despite the prevailing feeling of unrest, the rebellion was finally initiated by a former advocate for the Union, John Erskine, Earl of Mar, largely in a fit of pique at being snubbed from the court of the new King George I.

After raising the standard on the Braes of Mar in early September, Mar began to march south, securing many supporters among Scotland's powerful landowners and gentry such as Lord Drummond and William Murray, Marquis of Tullibardine. As with many families, the Atholls had divided loyalties. Murray's father, the Duke of Atholl, remained loyal to the government as did his brothers James and Edward. However, his two younger brothers, Charles and George, the latter of whom was to play a key role in the 1745 Rising, supported the Jacobites. By the end of the month Mar, with a 5,000 strong army, marched into Perth, which had been taken two weeks previously by Colonel John Hay of Cromlix, son of the Earl of Kinnoull. The city magistrates, hearing of the Jacobite advance, had appealed for help and gathered some support from the Duke of Atholl and the Sheriff and Lord Lieutenant of Fife who sent a small number of men. However, in the event little resistance was offered. The Athollmen joined the Jacobite forces, the Fife troops fled and the inhabitants of Perth were forced to swear an oath to James Francis Stuart ('The Old Pretender') or risk banishment from the town.

The town was heavily fortified by a line of entrenchments broken at intervals by triangular projections, or redans, which allowed slanting fire towards attackers and the old Cromwellian fort on the South Inch was re-occupied. It is not entirely clear the extent to which the defences would have been effective. The moat of the Cromwellian fort was re-filled by cutting a trench from the Craigie burn but it was in a ruinous state. Lewis Petit's 1716 Plan of Perth with the retrenchment made about it by

*Oath of Allegiance to*
*James Francis Stuart (James VIII)*
*by the people of Perth*
*(Perth & Kinross Council Archive)*

the Pretenders' Engineers shows that the north east bastion had collapsed and documentary evidence suggests that stonework had intermittently been removed since its abandonment in 1660.[1] Further, a Jacobite commander claimed that the line of entrenchments was so badly constructed that it became the 'jest of the hostile army'.[2] In the event, the defences were never put to the test. After the indecisive Battle of Sheriffmuir, Mar had retreated to Perth and although James Francis finally joined him there in January, the rebellion was effectively over. The English Jacobites had been crushed following the Battle of Preston and the Hanoverian army was steadily increasing with re-enforcements arriving from Holland and Ireland. On hearing of the opposition's advance on Perth, the Jacobites fled and retreated north, burning a number of Perthshire villages such as Auchterarder, Blackford, Crieff and Dunning to impede the government army's advance. By February James Francis was on his way back to France along with Mar. Neither was ever to return to Scotland.

The 1715 Rising had clearly shown to the government the level of discontent of many of the Scottish population toward the Hanoverian regime and serious consideration was given on how best to secure the country. Estates were fortified, cities and towns throughout Scotland were heavily garrisoned and four permanent Highland barracks were planned. For Perth's role in the rebellion, a massive pentagonal fortress commanding the town from the high ground to the north west of the city was planned but never realised. These were immediate solutions, enthusiasm for which largely waned over time. However, 10 years later, interest in securing Scotland by military means was to be re-ignited, essentially by Simon Fraser, 11th Lord Lovat.

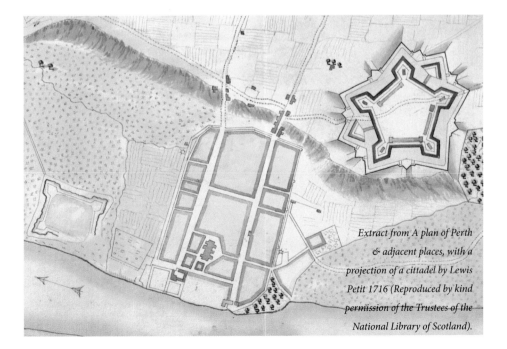

*Extract from A plan of Perth & adjacent places, with a projection of a cittadel by Lewis Petit 1716 (Reproduced by kind permission of the Trustees of the National Library of Scotland).*

SIMON LORD LOVAT.

Aliamet sculp

Portrait of Simon Fraser, 11th Lord Lovat. The axe and funeral mask refer to Lovat's eventual demise (Reproduced by kind permission of the Trustees of the National Library of Scotland).

# General Wade in Scotland

*Lord grant that Marshal Wade*
*May by thy mighty aid*
*Victory bring.*
*May he sedition hush,*
*And like a torrent rush,*
*Rebellious Scots to crush.*
*God save the King!*
- Sixth verse of the National Anthem, said to have been first
performed in London, 1745

## Lord Lovat's letter

It is unlikely that General Wade would ever have seen service in Scotland had it not been for the political agitations of Simon Fraser, 11th Lord Lovat. Lovat was clan chief of the Frasers with his ancestral seat and estates in Inverness-shire and came to have the unenviable epithets of the 'Spider of Dounie' and 'the most devious man in Scotland' largely due to his political double dealing. By the time of Lovat's memorandum to King George I in 1724, he had already been exiled to France where he had converted to Catholicism. He returned to Scotland on a Jacobite mission, which he promptly betrayed to the London government, leading to his imprisonment in France for treachery until his escape in 1713.

In his letter, Lovat wrote that the Highlands were rife with violence, extortion and thievery and that measures put into place by the government to control the Highlands after the 1715 rebellion had not been successful. In particular, he points to the Disarming Act of 1716 that disallowed Highlanders from carrying all 'warlike' weapons. Of course, such an Act proved difficult to enforce and worse, Lovat suggested that it left loyalists vulnerable as they dutifully handed in their weapons while those disloyal to the king only handed in useless and broken weapons, thereby remaining armed. Further, the Highland barracks built at great expense by the government were all but useless as they were wrongly sited and manned by regular troops who were unused to the rugged and mountainous terrain of the Highlands so could not pursue criminals and bring them to justice. Unlike, of course, the Independent Companies who were made up of Highlanders under the command of 'gentlemen of good affection and of credit in that country'.[3] However, the Independent Companies had been disbanded in 1717 as a waste of money. Lovat had been a commander of one of the disbanded Companies and the intention of his letter appears to have been largely to recoup some of the fiscal and social status that he had lost as a result. His account, however, disturbed the government enough to institute an enquiry and in July 1724 Wade departed to Scotland with a brief to ascertain how much truth there was in Lovat's memorandum and to make recommendations on how to best settle that part of the country. His report reached King George on 10th December. It largely supported Lovat's claims and, crucially, declared that of the 22,000 men in the Highlands capable of bearing arms, only 10,000 were loyal to the king. The rest had been actively involved in rebellion and would happily rise again in support of the Pretender.[4] The government's response to this news was swift and on 24th December Wade was made Commander in Chief, North Britain and dispatched to Scotland the following year to make good his recommendations.

## Wade's proposals to best settle the Highlands

By the time he arrived in Scotland Wade had already had a distinguished army career. In 1690, at the age of 17, he had joined the British army as an ensign, proving his military abilities at Flanders, Portugal and Spain. He moved rapidly through the ranks and by 1714 had been promoted to Major General and granted a colonelcy for exposing an apparent planned uprising supported by Sweden in 1717.

One of Wade's first acts in Scotland was to re-establish the Independent Companies, acknowledging their value in preventing disorder in the Highlands through their familiarity of the people, language and terrain. However, he proposed that this time the Companies should be under martial law as lack of proper regulation in the past had led to bribery and corruption especially among the commanders. He raised six companies, one of which was commanded by Lovat. These Companies were the early forerunner to the Black Watch (Royal Highland Regiment). He also implemented a new, more stringent Disarming Act with penalties equivalent to those of a felony such as transportation rather than the previous punishment of fines.[5]

Wade then began to put into place measures to effectively garrison Scotland. In 1727, he founded a fort named Fort George after the new king who had succeeded to the throne that same year. The fort made use of the remains of the old medieval castle which was situated 'within half a musket shot of the Bridge of Inverness'[6] This would allow government troops stationed at the fort to command this important river crossing, thereby preventing the rebels descending into the Lowlands. A new fort, named Fort Augustus in honour of King George II's third son William, Duke of Cumberland (later to be given the soubriquet 'The Butcher' in the aftermath of Culloden), supplanted the old barracks at Killiwhimmen. Wade notes in his 1724 proposals that the barracks were wrongly sited as they were too distant from Loch Ness and, being land locked, were not able to readily receive provisions in the event of a seige.[7] As at Inverness, Fort Augustus would control a key pass into the south and would also be equidistant from the already existing Fort William and the fort at Inverness. This would allow the governor of Fort Augustus, whom Wade intended to be chief of command of all three forts, to quickly assemble 1,000 men to march to any part of the Highlands to crush uprisings. The scale of Fort Augustus was ambitious and although founded in 1729 it was not fully completed until 1742. To keep open communication between his new forts at Inverness and Killiwhimmen, a ship called the Highland Galley was built on Loch Ness with room for a party of 50 or 60 soldiers.

No explicit proposals are made regarding the construction of roads in Wade's 1724 report to King George on the state of the Highlands, although he does note that the disadvantageous situation that the regular soldiers found themselves in due to the mountainous terrain was similar to that in the Sevennes in France and the Catalans in Spain. He also adds that the situation was made 'still more impractical for the want of roads and bridges'.[8] It is in his scheme delivered to the king in April 1725 that he requested money to improve the roads for better communication of the troops between forts and the barracks. However, it is not until January 1726, having already started work on the Fort William to Killiwhimmen road that he puts forward the suggestion of an annual sum of money for road construction and salary for a dedicated Inspector of Roads.[9] His request was granted and by 1730, Wade had a respectable annual budget of £3,000, although supplementary grants were often requested if costs were more than anticipated.[10]

## New ways through the Highlands

There were clearly roads in the Highlands prior to General Wade arriving and maps such as Herman Moll's *A Pocket Companion of ye Roads of ye North Part of Great Britain called Scotland 1718* show them to be fairly extensive.[11] However, many of the existing roads, described by the *Edinburgh Evening Courant* dated 17th November 1725 as 'hardly possible for a single man' would not have been fit for General Wade's purpose which was the rapid movement of troops and wheeled vehicles such as gun- and baggage- trains to and from isolated forts and barracks.

A start was made on the Fort William to Killiwhimmen road in 1725 and the following year he inspected the work, ordering it to be 'enlarged and carried on for wheeled carriage over the mountains on the south side of the Lake' to Inverness, thereby connecting the garrisons at Fort William, Killwhimmen and Inverness.[12] The road was completed in 1727, although Wade realigned a section of road in 1732 running it nearer the lochside from Foyer to Dores whereas previously it had taken the higher ground further inland.

Wade then turned his attention to creating and improving two major lines of north–south communication so that those troops stationed in major strongholds such as Stirling and Edinburgh and barracks such as Perth could be rapidly deployed to the Highlands should trouble arise. In 1728 he began his longest road, at 102 miles, which ran from Dunkeld to Inverness and, apart from 10 miles which he estimated would take 100 men a month or six weeks to perfect, he had completed it the following year.[13] It appears that Wade initially

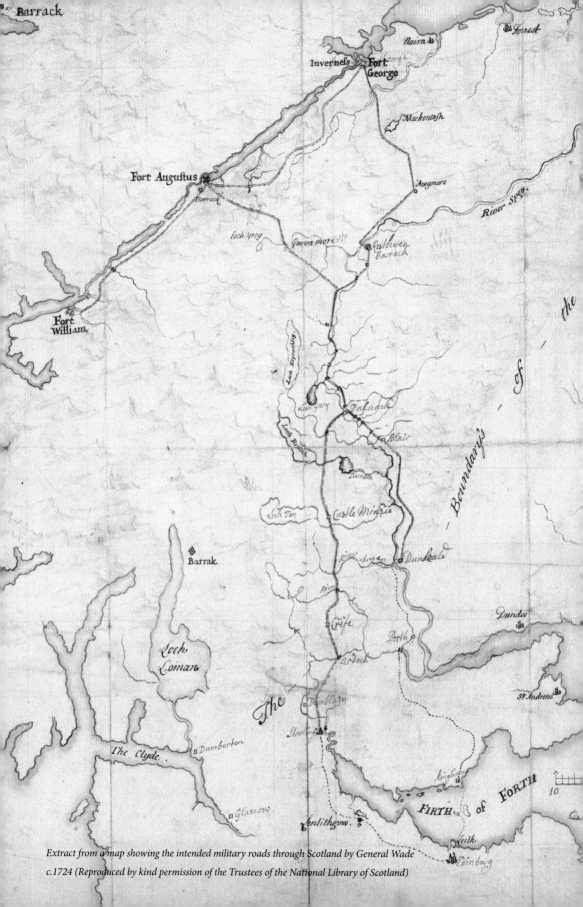

Barrack

Nairn

Inverness Fort George

S. Mackentosh

Forrest

Fort Augustus

Barrack

Aveymare

River Spey

loch Spey

Garva more

Ruthven Barrack

Fort William

Loch Erricht

Loch Garry

Dalnacle

Loch Rannoch

Blair

Tumel

Loch Tay

Castle Minzie

River Tummel

Dunkeld

Barrak

River

Amen

Crife

Ardoch

Perth

Dundee

Loch Loman

St Andrews

The Clyde

Dumbarton

The

Dunblane

Starling

Boundary's of the

FIRTH of FORTH

kinghn

Glascow

Linlithgow

Leith

Edinburg

10

*Extract from a map showing the intended military roads through Scotland by General Wade*
*c.1724 (Reproduced by kind permission of the Trustees of the National Library of Scotland)*

planned the road to extend further south. In a letter to Lord Townsend dated July 1727, Wade suggests that now the Fort William to Inverness road had been made practicable for the march of troops, cannon and other wheeled carriages, it 'may be continued to Perth at very moderate expense by the Regiments quartered in these parts'.[14] In the event, Wade did not carry out any improvements on the existing Inver to Perth Road. Neither did he bridge the River Tay, although tradition holds that this was his intention but one which he abandoned after receiving a cool reception from the Duke of Atholl. The lack of bridge at this point meant that the troops using this road would have to rely on the ferries at Inver to cross the Tay. From Dunkeld, Wade more or less followed the existing route north via Moulinearn, following the steep western bank through the Pass of Killiecrankie to Blair Atholl. At Blair he chose not to improve the long established route from Blair to Ruthven Barracks by way of the Minigaig Pass but instead followed the considerably lower lying river valleys via the Pass of Drumochter. The Minigaig was most likely avoided due to the height of the hills over which the existing road crossed and so the extremely bad weather it would suffer during the winter. It was still used as a shortcut, at least until 1745, when it is said that an entire company of Hanoverian soldiers was lost due to adverse weather while making its way to Strathspey.

Preparation for his next road took place in 1729 while finishing the season's work on the Dunkeld to Inverness route. In a letter to Duncan Forbes dated 2nd October the same year Wade describes how before retiring to his 'hutt' at Dalnacardoch for the night he had joined the soldiers working on the road in a feast of four oxen which they had prepared. He also partook in plenty of 'bumpers' (seemingly Wade's term for getting very drunk) from which it had taken five days to 'sett' him on his 'leggs again'.[15] This had allowed him to take a second survey of the projected road between Crieff to Dalnacardoch, which would be the following year's work. The *Edinburgh Evening Courant* dated 9th October 1729 reported that the bridge at which the festivities had taken place had been called Oxbridge, opposite Loch Garry. It has been suggested that the collapsed bridge of which only the abutments now survive and which would have crossed the Allt Coire Mhic-Sith Burn is where the feast took place. A map by Wade of the intended military roads shows that he considered starting his road to Dalnacardoch from Stirling.[16] However, it transpired that he did not do this, instead starting his road from Crieff. It was his successor Major Caulfeild who eventually improved this road between 1741 and 1742, by which time Wade had left Scotland. From Crieff the road passed through the Sma' Glen and Glen Cochill to Aberfeldy, skirting the western end of Loch Tummel before passing through Glen Errochty via Trinafour. From here, Wade negotiated the steep climb to Dalancardoch by using a series of traverses, as was his standard method for sharp ascents. The Crieff to Dalnacardoch road was started and completed in 1730 and totalled 43 miles.

Finally, Wade connected to his new Fort Augustus in 1731 by branching off the Dunkeld to Inverness route at Dalwhinnie, a stretch of 28 miles. The Dalwhinnie to Fort Augustus road is the last road for which we have clear evidence of Wade's construction, although it is often suggested that he was responsible for a cross route from Crubenbeag to Catlodge. On 30th October, to celebrate the king's birthday and the completion of the Dalwhinnie road which had been held up for six weeks due to continual rain, Wade organised a feast for the six parties of soldiers, including a party from the newly established Independent Companies.

Wade spent the next eight working seasons perfecting his military system by continuing to strengthen major strongholds such as Dumbarton, Edinburgh and Stirling and realigning sections of roads where necessary. In addition, some bridges on the road network still had to be built. He finally left Scotland in 1740 and was succeeded as Commander in Chief by Lieutenant General Clayton. However, before he left he entrusted his road building programme to Major William Caulfeild and it was to be under Caulfeild that the military infrastructure conceived by Wade was finally put to the test.

# Wade, Caulfeild and the '45

*'And pray, who so fit to lead forth this parade,*
*As the babe of Tangier, my old grandmother Wade?*
*Whose cunning's so quick but whose motions so slow,*
*That the rebels march on while he's stuck in the snow'*
-Verse from the seditious *God Prosper our King*

## Jacobitism resurrected

Caulfeild appears to have been with General Wade from at least 1729 when he writes a receipt from Dalnacardoch, Wade's headquarters during the work on the Dunkeld to Inverness road, for bed plaids for road working parties.[17] By 1732 he was a subaltern overseeing a party of road builders and appointed Inspector of Roads the same year. Following Wade's departure, Caulfeild supervised the improvement of the Crieff to Stirling road in 1741–42 which General Clayton noted was in such a bad state that it would not be able to carry troops or artillery should the need arise.[18] A start was also made on the Dumbarton to Inveraray road in 1744 but this was abruptly halted following news of Charles Edward Stuart's (Bonnie Prince Charlie) arrival in Scotland in July the following year.

Since the 1715 Rising, the desire to restore the Stuarts to the throne had waned in the face of the increased prosperity that the Union had seemingly brought, especially to powerful landowners. However, in 1739 interest in the Jacobite cause was once again revived. Open hostilities had started between Britain and Spain and there were suggestions of a potential war with France. The same year a group of influential noblemen and gentry formed the Association of Jacobite Sympathisers. The association included Donald Cameron of Lochiel whose father had come out for Mar in 1715, James Drummond, 3rd Duke of Perth whose father had supported the Stuarts in both 1689 and 1715, his uncle Lord John Drummond and Lord Lovat. Lovat by this point had once again fallen out of favour with the Hanoverian regime in Scotland when General Wade had stripped him of his Independent Company on suspicion of stealing the soldiers' pay.

*Caulfeild's receipt from Dalnacardoch dated 1729*
*(from National Records of Scotland GD1/369/55)*

*Prince Charles Edward*
*Stuart ('Wanted Poster') by*
*Richard Cooper (Scottish*
*National Portrait Gallery)*

The association had promised to raise men in support of the Stuarts but only if French backing was forthcoming, which appeared increasingly unlikely after French victories over Britain in May 1745. Undeterred, the Prince decided to go it alone, landing on Eriskay in July 1745. The news of the Prince's arrival without men, arms or money was initially met with alarm among his supporters but when the standard was raised at Glenfinnan on 19th August the Prince had managed to assemble more than 1,000 men and had garnered the support of leading clan chiefs. Making good use of General Wade's roads the Prince began his march into the Lowlands, past the Highland barracks and forts so recently established but now so undermanned that they were powerless to stop the Jacobite troops.

The same day on which the Stuart standard was raised, Lieutenant General Sir John Cope, who had replaced Clayton as Commander in Chief in Scotland, started to make his way north to meet the Jacobite force. The army at his disposal was in a poor state and he eventually rode out with 2,000 men, about half of that which was available to him. Most of the Hanoverian troops were in Flanders, including the Independent Companies established by Wade (now the 43rd Foot). With the road building programme temporarily come to an end, Major William Caulfeild had been appointed Cope's Quartermaster General. Using the Stirling to Dalnacardoch road, Cope reached Dalwhinnie where he was informed that the Jacobite army was marching to meet them at the Corrieyairack Pass. General Wade had chosen to construct his road over the Corrieyairack as the only suitable way through the Monadhliath Mountains. As was his standard construction method, Wade had negotiated the steep ascent by 17 traverses, each of which was commanded by that above it, giving the descending Jacobite army a firm advantage. Further, promised local support had not materialised and the Jacobite army was thought to outnumber Cope's own. He decided not to attempt to force the Pass, instead taking the other branch of the military road to Inverness, allowing the Jacobite army to move southwards into Perthshire unchecked. The Prince entered Perth in early September, an advance party having already secured the city, where he was joined by a number of leading Jacobites including Lord George Murray of the Atholl family and James Drummond, both of whom were made Lieutenant Generals of the Jacobite army.

The Prince stayed just over a week in Perth before marching out for Edinburgh where Cope was also headed, having ordered shipping to return his troops to the city as soon as he had reached Inverness. By the time the Prince was marching triumphantly into the city, Cope and his army had only just reached Dunbar. Without a substantial garrison, the city had fallen quickly, although the castle remained with the government troops. The two armies finally met at Prestonpans on the 21st September and Cope was soundly defeated in less than 10 minutes. The Prince was now eager to march on England.

Extract of a map showing Wade's movements through
England as he attempted to intercept the Jacobite
army (© The British Library Board (292.c.29))

## Wade: Back to the battlefield

Since leaving Scotland General Wade had been given joint command of the Anglo-Austrian force in Flanders in 1743, applying for leave due to ill heath the following year and soon after resigning from his post. In 1745, at 72 years of age, he was brought out of retirement, appointed Commander in Chief of the government troops and ordered to check the descending Jacobite army. After assembling at Newcastle, Wade began to march to Scotland but at Morpeth he learnt that the Jacobite army was making its way to Peebles and correctly predicted that it was heading towards Carlisle. The Jacobite troops who had been marching to meet them on an eastward route by way of Kelso had been a diversionary tactic. Wade fell back to Newcastle, finally marching his troops over a westward road to Carlisle. However, unlike those he had constructed in Scotland, the road to Carlisle was poor and unfit for the march of troops, baggage trains and artillery. The troops were not well provisioned, the weather treacherous and at Hexham, Wade once again decided to turn back to Newcastle.

The Prince and his army arrived in Derby in December. It had been just under five months since the Prince had set foot on Scottish soil and with great successes behind him he was ready to march on London. However, Lord George Murray advised caution. He argued that Cumberland and Wade's more experienced armies were rapidly advancing on them and a third army defended London. In fact, the armies were further away and less organised than Lord George thought. Still, support from the English Jacobites, which would have made such a move successful, had not been forthcoming. Lord George's preferred option was to tactically retreat, overwinter in Scotland and draw more recruits. The Prince conceded, although only when a number of officers backed Lord George. Wade once again attempted to intercept the Jacobite army as they marched along the west side of the Pennines but had only reached Wakefield whilst the Prince was at Wigan, several days' march away. Realising that his troops were now unlikely to gain on the Prince's, he sent 4,000 of the fittest men across the Pennines to Penrith but recalled the order due to bad weather. At Newcastle Wade was relieved of his post. The Prince entered Scotland unchecked and achieved another victory over the Hanoverian forces at Falkirk on 17th January 1746, after which Cumberland took command of the government forces. Following a Council of War at Crieff, the Prince and his army began to make their way once again into the Highlands heading for Inverness, with the Prince taking the Crieff to Dalnacardoch road and sending his artillery along the easier Dunkeld road.

The final battle was fought on Culloden Moor on 16th April 1746. The Jacobite troops, outnumbered and exhausted by a night march, proved to be no match for Cumberland's well organised army. Lord George and the remnants of the Jacobite army assembled at Ruthven ready to continue the battle but the fight was over for the Prince. He sent a message for them to disperse and to seek their safety, later escaping to France.

*This is the Butcher beware of your Sheep.*

*A contemporary engraving showing the Duke of Cumberland tearing the flesh off a tired and ragged Highlander (Reproduced by kind permission of the Trustees of the National Library of Scotland).*

## The Aftermath

Eager to ensure that the Jacobites would never again pose a military threat, Cumberland's reprisals were ruthless and indiscriminate. Anyone suspected of Jacobite sympathies was executed or imprisoned including those noblemen who had not managed to escape to the continent. Despite not actively taking much part in the Rising, Lovat was found guilty of treason and beheaded. He was the last man executed at Tower Hill in London. Estates were forfeited and another Disarming Act was put into place, this time not only banning weaponry but also plaid and the playing of bagpipes. Scotland was once again heavily garrisoned and by September there were over 15,000 government troops in Scotland. This did not abate until General Humphrey Bland was appointed the new Commander in Chief of North Britain in 1747. Plans were once again drawn up to provide the increased number of Hanoverian forces with bases in the Highlands, after the humiliating sight of the forts along the Great Glen falling so easily to the Jacobite forces on their retreat north. Only Fort William did not fall despite a lengthy siege. Fort Augustus was repaired but the fort at Inverness was abandoned and replaced by Fort George on Ardersier Point. This new fort took 21 years to complete, by which time the Highlands were finally peaceful.

## The Highlands laid open

Along with a military survey initiated in 1747, the road building programme once again became a priority so that 'a country so very inaccessible by nature should be thoroughly explored and laid open'.[19] Major Caulfeild resumed his post as Inspector of Roads. To help him with his work he was assigned four engineers in 1749, a year which also saw a massive deployment of men working on the roads: approximately 1,350 from five different regiments.[20]

Under Caulfeild's supervision, two further main roads running from south to north through the Highlands were constructed. The first took a westerly route from Stirling to Fort William and the second ran from Blairgowrie to Braemar, eventually extending to Coupar Angus and Fort George on Ardersier Point. A warrant to provide Major Caulfeild with gunpowder to make this road was issued to the Officer Command of the Train at Perth in July 1748, and work on the road was also started this year by General Handasyd's Regiment.[21] The following year, 300 men from the Welsh Fusiliers were sent to start work on the road from Blairgowrie and another 300 from General Guise's regiment were ordered to work southward from Braemar, the intention being that both parties should meet at the Spittal of Glenshee. However, at the season's end General Guise's detachment had stopped approximately two and a half miles to the north of the Spittal and the Blairgowrie party had only reached Dalrulzion. It was not until 1750 that the six remaining miles were completed.[22] Over the next six or so years, work was intermittently carried out to extend the road to Ardersier Point. To the south from Blairgowrie there was already '13 good miles of good road to Perth through a fine country'.[23] So, in effect, by 1757 there was a road connecting Perth to the new Fort George.

*The military road (now largely overlain by the modern road) following the lower lying valleys of Gleann Beag in Perthshire.*

A further road from Blairgowrie to Coupar Angus was also constructed which would have improved communication with Dundee. This road is not shown on General Roy's military survey or Dorret's map of 1750 but there is mention of repair by the Commissioners of Supply in 1758.[24] Any road that did exist, however, was not deemed suitable for military purpose, leading Caulfeild to state in a letter dated 1766 to the commissioners that the bridge of Isla built the previous year would be inaccessible to wheeled carriages until a road was built on either side of it. The road must have been improved to military standards at some point soon after as by 1770 annual repair work was being carried out by military parties.

The cross routes connecting Amulree to Dunkeld and to Coupar Angus, and thereby the three main north–south lines of communication running through Perthshire, are also commonly referred to as being military. It is not entirely clear when the Dunkeld to Coupar Angus Road was built or by whom. It does not feature on General Roy's Military Survey but must have been in existence by 1753 as, in that year, there is a petition for road repairs recorded in the Minutes of the Commissioners of Supply for Perthshire.[25] This would also indicate that at this time, maintenance of the road was largely a matter for the county rather than the army. From the late 18th century, however, the road frequently appears on military lists.

The road connecting Dunkeld to Amulree running from Inver through Strathbraan to Newton of Ballinreigh was in existence from at least 1735 but there appears to be little evidence of military contribution until 1747 when Commissioners of Supply agreed to provide transport and services with regard to replacement or repair of a bridge over the Braan.[26] By 1761, the military was carrying out annual repair and maintenance work.

In terms of overall mileage, Caulfeild greatly increased the road system through Scotland, supervising and planning the construction of approximately 800 miles to General Wade's 240 miles. He held his position as Inspector of Roads until his death in 1767.

# The King's Roads

*The old ways (for roads I shall not call them) consisted chiefly
of stony moors, bogs, rugged rapid fords, declivity of hills,
entangling woods and giddy precipices. You will say this is a dreadful
catalogue to be read to him about to take a Highland journey*
- Edmund Burt

## Surveying the land and other preparations

*A military draftsman shown on A prospect of that part of the land and sea adjacent to ye
barrack to be built in Glen Elg by John Bastide, 1720 (Reproduced by kind permission of the
Trustees of the National Library of Scotland)*

There was very little in the way of detailed mapping of the Highlands before General
Wade's time so prior to constructing the roads, he and his surveyors would make sketches
and plans of the ground to be covered the following year, noting the condition of any
existing roads and the work necessary to make them suitable for wheeled vehicles. Such
detail can be seen on the *Sketch and description of the proposed Roads from Callander and
Loch Tay to Fort William and Appin including details of mileage and of inns.*[27] The ground
conditions, boggy or dry, were also noted, as were any steep ascents, precipices, existing
bridges and other suitable points to cross rivers. It was not until after the rebellion of 1745,
that a survey to provide complete and uniform coverage of Scotland was deemed essential
in order to open up such an inaccessible and remote area as the Highlands.

*Surveying in the Highlands, a view near Loch Rannoch by Paul Sandby, 1749. The surveyor is looking down the alidade of a theodolite while two soldiers measure with chains. In the very background, a soldier stands with a flag to mark the backstation while another soldier carries a flag to the forestation (© The British Library Board (K.Top.50.83.2))*

The initiator of the survey was Colonel David Watson, an engineering officer and Deputy Quartermaster General who had been frustrated with the lack of reliable mapping when with a detachment working on the roads and setting up military posts. He promoted the idea to the Duke of Cumberland and by 1747 the survey was underway. Watson remained director of the survey until 1754, although most of the practical work was carried out by William Roy. Roy was assisted by six surveying parties, each of which comprised a non-commissioned officer and six soldiers under the guidance of an engineer. The use of soldiers in survey work was not unusual and a precedent had already been set during the land survey of Ireland in 1654–6 which used soldiers as they were able to 'wade through bogs and water, climb rocks, fare lodge hard'.[28] In each survey party, one carried the theodolite, two measured with the chain of 45 or 50 feet in length, two for the fore and back stations and the remaining one acted as batman. Rather than triangulation, the survey was based on a series of measured traverses along main features such as rivers and roads using the theodolite to measure angles and the chains for distances. The surveys were carried out during the summer and the maps drawn over the winter in the Board of Ordnance offices in Edinburgh. The initial aim of the survey had been to map only the Highlands but when this was largely completed in 1752, the work was extended into the Lowlands. Although curtailed when war with France appeared imminent and the engineers and soldiers were required elsewhere, by 1755, in just nine years, Roy and his men had completed the first uniform large scale map of the Scottish mainland.

Apart from the survey, many other preparations were necessary prior to constructing a military road. A wide variety of tools and ordnance were ordered in advance from the Tower of London and transported to Scotland by sloop. In 1730 the tools ordered for carrying on the roads in the Highlands included iron spades, iron and wooden shovels, pick axes, sledge hammers, hand screws, iron crowbars, wheelbarrows and hand barrows. A terse note at the end of the order reminds the storekeeper that as 'the work for the most part will be carried on in stony and rocky ground, tools of a proportional strength are needed than those delivered out of the stores last year'.[29] Gunpowder was also used regularly.

The line of the road also had to be set out before the main working party started construction. This was the responsibility of an advance party of a subaltern and about 20 to 30 men who would mark out the road on the ground using two lines of camp colours (flags). Wade preferred the road to run in straight lines where possible as this lessened the distance between two points. Hills were negotiated by following the contour, although steep slopes were avoided where possible as a retaining wall would have to be built to prevent earth and stone from the broken bank falling onto the road. The building of retaining walls was considered both 'tedious and expensive' and so preference was given to lower lying ground if it was not too boggy.[30] As previously mentioned, steep ascents were negotiated using traverses.

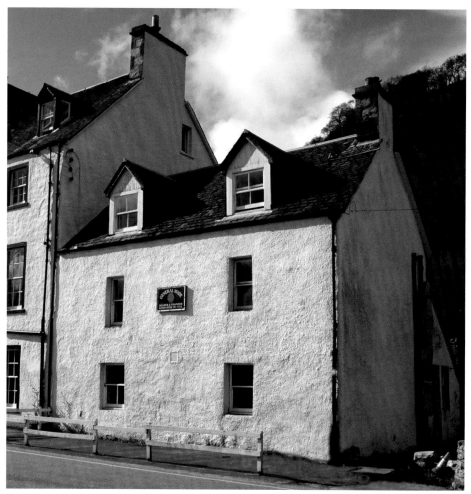

*General Wade's 'hutt' in Weem where he stayed to oversee the construction of the Tay Bridge, Aberfeldy. The first and second stories are the original portions but the attic and dormer windows have been added later.*

The advance party would also set up blacksmiths forges and assemble camps for the soldiers every 10 miles or so along the road. Under General Wade, the soldiers usually lived in hutted accommodation many of which later developed into inns called kingshouses as they were on the king's way (road).

There is some evidence to suggest that the preferred 'hut' to convert into an inn was the general's rather than the soldiers', the former no doubt being much more salubrious. The soldiers' accommodation often appears to have been used for more mundane purposes such as sheiling bothies. The kingshouses in Perthshire would have included those at Tummel Bridge, Dalnacardoch and Moulinearn (now all private dwellings) and at Weem. Later in Caulfeild's time it was far more common for the soldiers to spend the nights under canvas. In Lowland areas soldiers could be lodged with civilians.

*Soldiers erecting a tent from an image entitled Scenes from the camp on Hampton Green, unattributed, 1731 (© National Museums of Scotland)*

## Organising the workforce

The military predominantly provided the workforce and finance for road building, although specialist craftsmen such as masons, pavers, carpenters and blacksmiths would have been civilians. Eventually there came to be much more cooperation between the military and the counties, particularly in Caulfeild's time and civilian assistance would be offered such as the provision of carts and horses, civil labour and funds. In the early days, however, Wade and his men were largely on their own.

Generally, the soldiers worked only during the summer months from the start of April to the end of October with the number of the men working on the road, at least in Wade's time, varying from 300 to no more than 500 men. Work on the road system increased after the 1745 Rebellion and Caulfeild adapted this schedule as required, occasionally lengthening the working season as on the Dumbarton to Inverary road which was extended over Christmas. On other occasions he increased the number of men but shortened the work period to as little as 92 days running from the middle of June to the middle of September. The soldiers were organised in working parties typically comprising a captain, two subalterns, two sergeants, two corporals, one drummer and 100 men. The working parties were under the command and direction of the subalterns, although the non-commissioned officers were the immediate overseers of the work.

*Reconstruction showing the soldiers building a section of road near Amulree (artist: David Hogg).*

For their efforts, the men working on the road received six pence per day over and above their pay as soldiers; a corporal and a drummer were allowed eight pence and a sergeant received a shilling. However, if the weather was bad and the men were unable to work, they received no extra pay. The subalterns received two shillings and six pence per day to compensate their initial outlay in building huts and supplying provisions such as food and clothes. Captains, however, received no extra pay as they were sent out with the working party to keep the men in good order by holding court martial where necessary and meting out suitable punishments.[31] The extra allowance that General Wade persuaded the government to pay the soldiers was generous but the labour would have been hard. In Caulfeild's time the work rate expected by the men was one and half yards (just less than 1.5m) per man per day, although Colonel Rickson apparently managed to increase this to two yards per day. Neither did the rate of pay increase. By 1760, the pay for civilian craftsmen who had been receiving a shilling under Wade had been raised by six pence but the soldiers' pay remained the same.

Orders issued by General Bland in 1754 set down the procedure for the payments of troops. The commanding officer of each working party was to produce a weekly report noting the numbers and rank of men in their party, the days and hours that his party or the men in it did not work and lengths of road completed. Based on this report, Major Caulfeild would work out the correct payment for each party and the commanding officer would divvy this out after deducting any expenses for necessaries that had been provided in advance. It was also made clear that the soldiers were not to be paid more than their subsistence until the work on the road had been completed and there would be strict punishments for those who kept a suttler (a camp follower who peddled provisions to the soldiers) and allowed the men to get into debt.[32]

## Constructing the roads

Once the necessary preparations had been carried out, soldiers from regiments stationed in the Highlands would leave their garrisons to begin construction work. Edmund Burt in *Letters from a Gentleman in the North of Scotland to his Friend in London* gives a very good contemporary account of road construction. His letter regarding the road is written in approximately 1737 so the information he gives relates to the methods used by General Wade. There is little archaeological or documentary evidence to suggest that basic construction techniques were substantially different under Caulfeild.

In general, soldiers would dig the road foundations, excavating the loose material until they reached a firm base of rock or gravel. The hollow would be filled with a layer of large stones, then smaller stones to fill up any gaps and finally topped with a thick layer of gravel to form a smooth and binding surface. Banks, formed from the excavated material, lined the road and separated the carriageway from the ditches. On hills, the ditches were of particular importance as they collected and conveyed water from the higher to lower slopes by means of a sunken and paved drain across the road surface. Underground culverts also appear to have been made use of and two well-preserved examples were revealed on a portion of the military road between Dalnacardoch to Dalnamein as part of an archaeological evaluation by Glasgow University Archaeology Department (GUARD) in 2010. The covered dry stone culverts ran underneath the road and in both cases they had been constructed at a slight downward angle, extending more than a metre beyond the surface of the road. The main purpose of the drainage was to prevent the surface of the road being washed away, although maintenance schedules show that re-gravelling was almost a yearly occurrence. The problem of erosion, however, appears to have been exacerbated by human agency. In a report to accompany surveys undertaken on parts of the Coupar Angus to Fort George road, Caulfeild complains that however well made the road, it would soon be destroyed if some method was not found or some law made that would prevent the trailing of timber or deal boards (a wheelless platform used to transport goods). This practice, he continues, made channels in the gravel which filled with rainwater, gathered into currents destroying all before them.[33] Perthshire appears to have been a particular culprit and an order had already been issued reminding people that the roads were for wheeled vehicles, not for deals or trees. Wade also specified that the breadth of the roads was to be standardised at 16 feet (4.8m) although they could be wider in areas where there were 'no expensive difficulties'.[34]

*A contemporary drawing by Paul Sandby entitled road builders shifting boulders (National Gallery of Scotland).*

This standardised method of construction was not always adhered to and would vary according to the material at hand or terrain the road was to cross. A watching brief carried out on a section of road constructed under the supervision of Caulfeild between Kingshouse and Altnafeadh revealed that the military road comprised solely of 300mm of gravel laid directly on peat and no trace of the specified layers of stones designed to give the road a firm foundation. The archaeologist suggested that this might be a lapse in standards on the part of the roadmakers or a paucity of infill material in the immediate locality.[35] The material for the roads would not have been imported from any great distance; rather the soldiers would use field boulders which could be broken and gravel quarried from the hillside. Many of these quarries still remain visible along the side of the roads. Burt also mentions possible solutions to the lack of infill material. In a very boggy area where there were no loose stones but trees were nearby, the road would be built of timber and fascines topped with gravel dug out of a nearby hill. Where the road ran through rocky passes or along cliff faces gunpowder would be used. Burt describes the operation on the section of road above Loch Ness. Miners would hang by ropes from the precipice over the water to bore holes into the rock face, which would then be filled with gunpowder and the stone blown away. Where the drop was great, stone walls would be built to prevent falls, especially of the carriages. Gunpowder was also used to remove any obstacles in the line of the road such as the fallen rock at Slochd Mor or, less spectacularly but probably more commonly, boulders and large stones were removed by the soldiers using levers and jacks and placed along the side of the road to use as markers in the snow.

*Boulders acting as snow markers along a section of road near Corrymuckloch in Perthshire*

Burt tells of the latter operation when soldiers encountered a large boulder when building the road through Glen Almond. After, wrenching out the boulder from the line of the road using levers and jacks they discovered some ashes and bones and half-burnt stalks of heath contained in a small container of square flat stones. Taking into account their proximity to a Roman fort and working under the assumption that the natives of the country could not have had the engineering knowledge to move the stone, the soldiers assumed that the cremated remains must be that of a Roman officer. The soldiers planned to keep the remains as a curiosity but on hearing of the incident, the Highlanders formed a solemn procession, gathered up the remains and reburied them firing their muskets over the new grave. The stone is traditionally thought to be the so called Ossian's Stone in the Sma' Glen.

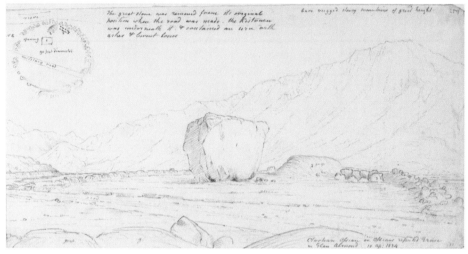

*Sketch of the stone under which a cremation is reputed to have been found by General Wade's road builders (© Courtesy of RCAHMS (Society of Antiquaries of Scotland Collection) Licensor www.rcahms.gov.uk. We are grateful to the Society of Antiquaries of Scotland for permission to reproduce this image).*

Finally, milestones, figured and painted, would have been erected every five miles along the road. Although not in its original position one of these markers, known as the Wade Stone, survives in Perthshire. The stone was erected during the construction of the Dunkeld to Inverness road and bears the contemporary carving of the date 1729. Salmond tells of a local tradition in which General Wade placed a guinea on the top of the 8 foot stone and when he returned the following year the coin was still there.[36] This old tradition appears to have survived and the top of the stone is still home to a number of recent coins.

The soldiers' work did not only include the construction of new roads but maintenance of those previously built. In 1733, General Wade successfully petitioned the Treasury for an annual allowance of £400 to maintain the roads and keep them in good condition and this was increased in 1740 to £500.[37] Maintenance works could include re-gravelling, re-digging of ditches, widening and re-alignment of the roads. This budget, however, was not only spent on road works but also had to be stretched to include repair work on the bridges that formed an essential part of the Highland military infrastructure.

## Building bridges

Before the military investment into Scotland's infrastructure, the construction of bridges, as with the roads, would have been a matter for the Commissioners of Supply or individual landowners. As such their construction would have been intermittent. Without a bridge, the crossing of rivers, especially by foot, could be treacherous and there would have been long waits until the water had fallen to a potentially manageable level. Ferries were rare except on the wider rivers and even then their usefulness could be limited dependent on the size of the boat. In many cases, especially in the Highlands, the boats would only carry three or four people with no room for a horse, which would have to swim at the stern while someone held up its head by a halter or bridle. Burt writes that this was fine at first but if

*The ferry at Inver crossing the River Tay, Perthshire by Alexander Nasmyth c.1810 (© Crown copyright: UK Government Art Collection).*

the river was wide the horse would tire and in time 'they would turn themselves on to their sides and patiently suffer themselves to be dragged along'.[38] In effect, river crossings could severely hamper the quick and easy passage of troops. As this was the reason for which the roads had been designed, bridge building became a necessary aspect of securing Scotland. It was, however, a relatively expensive and time consuming aspect so Wade preferred initially to ford rivers, bridging them only where the torrents proved too strong.

If erecting a bridge proved unavoidable the work was carried out by civilian masons who would either be from the nearest local community or itinerant. In one letter dated 1756 David Frew, a mason and plasterer, requests Sir Ludovick Grant recommend him to Governor Caulfeild for work on some of the bridges in 'Glenalick' or 'the new road to Barnarie' after travelling to Fort George at Ardersier Point, Castle Grant in Speyside and then south to Newhall for work.[39] The construction of bridges appears to have largely been by contract, either directly with the masons or through the laird who would then subcontract the work. Only one bridge building contract survives under Wade's name. The contract, dated 25th July 1730, is between himself and John Stewart the Laird of Kynachan to build a bridge over the River Tummel at an agreed cost of £200. The Laird was to receive £50 on signing the contract and £150 on completion of the work, which was to be by the last day in October (the end of General Wade's working season). Wade also manages to write into the contact a very respectable 20 year warranty on the work to be upheld by the Laird.[40] By Caulfeild's time, contracts directly with the mason for one or more bridges on a road appear more common, with accounts including records of the Dunkeld masons Thomas Clark and James Robertson who were responsible for, respectively, nine bridges between Ardkinglas and Inverary and 19 bridges on the Braemar to Blairgowrie road.[41]

*Tummel Bridge 1854 (Courtesy of AK Bell Library, Local Studies Department)*

The bridges that survive today are all of masonry arch construction, although records of General Wade's expenditure show that at least two of the 35 bridges mentioned were of timber with stone abutments. The masons working on the bridges appear to have largely used traditional construction methods and techniques. In the Tummel contract, Wade gives general dimensions for the bridge and requests that it was to be well made, of good quality materials and easily passable for wheeled carriage or cannon. He does not, however, give any further direction as to building methods or design. A more distinctive style of bridge is generally associated with those built under the supervision Caulfeild and his four engineers and may be exemplified by the bridge at the Spittal of Glenshee. It has a gently sloping parapet rising to a peak above the crown, generally with lower arches to provide a wider span. Not all bridges built under the supervision of Caulfeild follow this pattern and earlier similar examples are not unknown. As with Wade it is likely that Caulfeild and his engineers would provide the masons with general dimensions and instructions based on their earlier survey results rather than any detailed written specifications.

*The bridge at Spittal of Glenshee, built in 1749, showing the distinctive sloping parapet characteristic of a bridge built under the supervision of Caulfeild.*

To construct a modest single arch bridge, the masons would have followed some basic principles. First there would be some excavation to remove loose or unstable material to provide a firm foundation for the bridge. Abutments were usually raised to the base of the arch, although in many instances a site would be chosen to allow at least one side of the arch to spring directly from bedrock. The arch would be built over a temporary timber frame called the centring which would define and support the arch barrel until the keystones were inserted. Once construction was completed, the timer frame would usually be dismantled and re-used where possible. In most military bridges of this period, the arch stones would be flat and irregularly shaped with mortar packed into the gaps for support. The spandrel walls would be built from rubble masonry, most often roughly dressed boulders and field gatherings, and between the walls would be a fill of earth and gravel from the earlier excavations. The main purpose of the fill would be to provide a solid foundation for the carriageway. Finally, a lime harling would be applied to act as a protective coating, although this does not survive today. As with the roads, the bridges also had to be maintained and repairs would regularly include re-pinning, re-pointing, replacement of copes and re-harling. In other instances, bridges had to be rebuilt, the most common cause for their collapse being the fast flowing torrents of rivers.

# Constructing a single arch bridge
## (artist: David Hogg)

*The banks are cleared to provide a firm foundation for the bridge and a temporary timber frame is erected*

*The timber frame supports the arch barrel until the keystone is inserted*

*A lime harling is applied to the bridge*

*The carriageway is gravelled*

## The Tay Bridge at Aberfeldy

In 1732, Wade wrote that it was an absolute necessity to build a road over the River Tay as it was one of the largest rivers in the Highlands and impassable during the rainy season.[42] This was undoubtedly true but whereas the majority of the bridges in the military road network were modest, inexpensive and utilitarian, the monumentality, expense and grandeur of the Tay Bridge would suggest that it was meant more as a memorial to General Wade's work in Scotland and as a symbol of Hanoverian might.

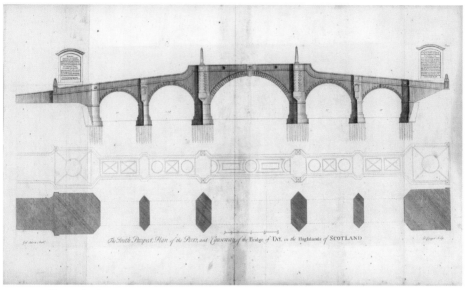

*William Adam's plan for the Tay Bridge (© Courtesy of RCAHMS. Licensor www.rcahms.gov.uk).*

*The Tay Bridge today*

The bridge was designed by William Adam, one of Scotland's foremost architects of the day, although Wade requested that the four distinctive obelisks which frame the centre arch be added. Instead of relying on local masons, master masons and other craftsmen such as carpenters were brought up from the north counties of England as Wade believed them to be more accustomed to works of a monumental nature. The bridge was constructed of grey chlorite schist with ashlar dressings and each of the five arches barrels comprised regularly cut and dressed voussoirs. The bridge is described in the House of Commons Journal of 1734 as being 'nearly 400 feet in length, the middle arch 60 feet wide, the starlings of oak, and the piers and landbreasts founded on piles shod with iron'. Mounted on the keystone of the middle arch is a marble panel bearing the monarchic symbol of a crown, sceptre and sword, and cannon detail on the elevation acts as a reminder of Hanoverian military strength. Further marble plaques on the upstream elevation bear inscriptions in Latin and English stating that, '…At the command of His Majesty King George II this bridge was erected in the year 1733. This with the road and other military works for securing a safe and easy communication between the Highlands and trading towns in the low country was…. committed to the care of Lieutenant General George Wade…who laid the first stone of the bridge on the 23rd of April and finished the work in the same year'. This is not strictly true as by the end of October, the end of the working season, the parapet was only completed up to a foot in height above the pavement with another three foot still to be completed along with the parapets.[43] The Tay Bridge cost £4095 5s 10d. To give some comparison, a single arch bridge of the type built under Wade could cost as little as £40. In a letter in the *King's Warrant Book XXX* Wade acknowledges that work was more expensive and time consuming than initially calculated, partly because the Justices of the Peace for Perthshire reneged on their promise to supply carriages for materials at the county's expense and problems with a free stone quarry.

*Symbols of Hanoverian military might: The crown, sword and sceptre. This plaque, along with the original Latin and English inscriptions were conserved in 2005 by Graciela Ainsworth (©Graciela Ainsworth); A cannon feature on the elevation of the bridge.*

The bridge also appears to have had problems with the foundations. In a report dated October 1784, Robert Reid noted that even before the masonry of the bridge was perfectly finished, it was acknowledged that the foundations had not been built deep enough. To remedy this, a dam was built using a row of piles with a quantity of stones just downstream of the bridge so that whatever 'gravel, stones or whatever stuff the river brings' it would raise the bed around the piers to the height of the dam.[44] Later, in 1819 in his less than complimentary description of the Tay Bridge, Robert Southey and the civil engineer Thomas Telford had gone into the bed of the river and examined the foundations and had found them to be very insecure.[44] It is possible that they were aware of Reid's report. Either way, the bridge still stands and it is a testament to the work of those who were involved in its construction that it is still in use today carrying traffic much heavier than originally intended. Wade considered the Tay Bridge as his greatest achievement of the road building programme, formally opening the bridge on 8th August 1735.

# Epilogue

*If you'd seen these roads before they were made
You'd lift up your hands and bless General Wade*
-couplet commonly attributed to Major Caulfeild

General George Wade died in 1748 and was buried in Westminster Abbey and, following the death of Major Caulfeild in 1767, the road building programme was taken over by Colonel Skene. However, by this time, the Jacobite threat had diminished and, as a result, interest in the upkeep of Scotland's military infrastructure faded. Garrisons were substantially scaled down, leaving few men to carry out work on the roads and use of soldier labour eventually came to an end in the last decade of the 18th century. The military also quickly extricated themselves from the financial burden of paying for the upkeep of the roads. The fiscal responsibility initially fell to the Parliament who gradually began the handing over of roads to the counties. Finally, in 1803, this position was formalised and a commission was set up by Act of Parliament to supervise the expenditure on the roads and bridges in the Highlands. Half of the cost for improvements to the infrastructure was borne by the government and the other half by those who would benefit, such as the counties or landowners.

General Wade and Major Caulfeild had provided the Highlands with the first planned and engineered roads. As with the forts and barracks, the roads had largely served their purpose. By the 19th century, the impetus for communications in the Highlands was industry and commerce and the military roads did not necessarily suit civilian requirements. As a result, some roads, or sections thereof, were abandoned and others were re-aligned. Those that were still useful were maintained and improved and eventually subsumed into the new communication system of parliamentary roads, canals and railways.

In many ways, the abandonment of the roads has meant that many sections still survive along with key historic sites of the period. In Perthshire, the Crieff to Dalnacardoch road is one of the best-preserved military roads in Scotland. Modern roads have followed the approximate line of General Wade's Dunkeld to Inverness and Major Caulfeild's Blairgowrie to Braemar roads but they can still be easily traversed by cycle or car and along the routes it is possible to find the remains of this important period in military history such as barracks, bridges, milestones and castles. Many have been mentioned in the booklet but there is more information in the companion map *General Wade's Legacy: exploring the 18th century military roads in Perthshire.*

# Notes

1  National Library of Scotland, MS.1647 Z.03/01d

2  'Memoirs of the insurrection in Scotland in 1715. By John, Master of Sinclair. From the original manuscript in the possession of the Earl of Rosslyn. With notes by Sir Walter Scott' ed. by J. MacKnight in *Abbotsford Club* 30 (1858)

3  Lord Lovat's memorial to King George concerning the state of the Highlands reprinted in full in Edmund Burt, *Letters from a Gentleman In the North of Scotland to His Friend in London*, (London, 1818) vol.ii, pp. 254-267

4  General Wade's report of his journey taken under royal instruction 1724 reprinted in full in *Historical Papers Relating to the Jacobite Period 1699–1750*, ed. by James Allardyce, (Aberdeen, 1895), vol.i, pp. 131-146

5  ibid., p. 142

6  General Wade's report of his journey taken under royal instruction from George II 1727 reprinted in full in *Historical Papers Relating to the Jacobite Period 1699–1750*, Allardyce, vol. i, p 163

7  Report of Wade's journey taken in pursuance of royal instruction by General George Wade 1724 in *Historical Papers Relating to the Jacobite Period 1699–1750*, ed. by Allardyce, vol.i, p. 141

8  ibid., p 149

9  General Wade's scheme delivered to the King in April 1725 in *Historical Papers Relating to the Jacobite Period 1699–1750*, ed. by Allardyce, vol.i, p 149; General Wade's report of his journey under royal instructions dated June 1725 reprinted in full in Burt, *Letters from a Gentleman In the North of Scotland to His Friend in London* vol.ii, pp. 254-267

10  *Calendar of Treasury Books and Papers*, ed. by William A Shaw, (London, 1897), vol. i, pp. 349-363

11  NLS, EMGB.6.1.35 (4)

12  NLS, MS 7187

13  ibid.

14  ibid.

15  *Culloden papers. Comprising an extensive and interesting correspondence from the year 1625 to 1748*, ed. by H.R. Duff, (London, 1815) p.111

16  NLS, Acc.10497 Wade. 58e

17  National Archives of Scotland, GD1/369/55

18  *Calendar of Treasury Books and Papers*, ed. by Shaw, vol.v pp. 501-601

19  William Roy, 'An Account of a Measurement of a base on Hounslow Heath' in *Philosophical Transactions of the Royal Society of London* (1785) p. 386

[20] National Archives, War Office 26/21

[21] NA, MR1/497

[22] NA, WO 26/21; NLS, MS. 16492.03/38a

[23] NA, MR1/497

[24] British Library, Maps, K. Top 48.25.1.a–f Please note that General Roy's military map is available to view on the national Library website http://www.nls.uk/; NLS, EMS.s.640

[25] Perth and Kinross Council Archives, CC1/1/1

[26] ibid.

[27] NLS Acc.10497 Wade.58m

[28] William Petty, *The History of Ireland, commonly called The Down Survey*, (Dublin, 1851) p 316

[29] An Account of working tools necessary for carrying the new roads of communication in the Highlands of Scotland, transcribed by John Kerr in The Atholl Experience vol. 8 (2) p. 50 held at PKC Archives

[30] NA MR1/479

[31] Burt, *Letters from a Gentleman In the North of Scotland to His Friend in London*, vol. ii, pp 277-305

[32] NA, WO26/21

[33] BL, Maps, K. Top.48.66.6

[34] Burt, *Letters from a Gentleman In the North of Scotland to His Friend in London*, vol. ii, p 285

[35] John Lewis, *Kingshouse–Altnafeadh military road: watching brief,* (unpublished fieldwork report, 2009)

[36] J. B. Salmond, *Wade in Scotland,* (Edinburgh, 1938) pp 224-226

[37] *Calendar of Treasury Books and Papers*, William A Shaw (ed) (London, 1897), vol. v, p 500

[38] Burt, *Letters from a Gentleman In the North of Scotland to His Friend in London*, vol. ii, p. 167

[39] NAS, GD248/177/4

[40] NAS, GD1/53/97

[41] NA, WO 26/27

[42] *Calendar of Treasury Books and Papers*, ed. by, vol. v, p. 406

[43] *More Culloden Papers*, ed. by Duncan Warrand, (Inverness, 1879) vol.iii, p 100

[44] Report of Robert Reid on the State of Coldstream Bridge in *Reports of the late John Smeaton FRS made on various occasions in the course of his employment as a civil engine*er, ed. by Longman, Hurst, Rees, Orme and Brown (London, 1813), vol. iii, p 248

[45] Robert Southey, *Journal of a Tour in Scotland* (London, 1929)

# Further Reading

Curtis, G. R. 1978-80, 'Roads and bridges in the Scottish Highlands: the route between Dunkeld and Inverness 1725-1925' in *Proceedings of the Society of Antiquaries of Scotland* Volume 110 pp. 475-496

Ruddock, T. Arch Bridges and their Builders 1735-1835, (Cambridge, Cambridge University Press)

Salmond, J. B. 1938, *Wade in Scotland*, (Edinburgh, The Dunedin Press Limited)

Skelton, R. A.1967, The Military Survey of Scotland (Edinburgh, Royal Scottish Geographical Society)

Tabraham, C. & Grove, D. 1997, *Fortress Scotland and the Jacobites,* (London, B.T. Batsford)

Taylor, W. 1976, *The military Roads in Scotland*, (Exeter; SRP Limited)

# Acknowledgements

This booklet is part of the three-year Bridging Perthshire's Past project, carried out by Perth and Kinross Heritage Trust between 2008-11 and supported by the Heritage Lottery Fund. During the course of the project I received invaluable assistance from too many people to list here, so these acknowledgements are restricted to those who assisted with the publication. Thanks are due to: Sara Ann Kelly and staff at A K Bell Library Local Studies department, Steve Connelly and staff at Perth and Kinross Council Archives, Chris Fleet and staff at the National Library of Scotland and Dr Carolyn Anderson for their assistance in sourcing primary documents and images; Alice Getley, Ian Hamilton, Katherine McBay and Sarah Winlow who provided comments and corrections; David Strachan for his advice and guidance; David Bowler, Andrew Driver, Derek Hall, Mark Hall, David Perry for providing comments and suggestion on the reconstruction drawings and to the artist, David Hogg. Special thanks are also due Lord Seafield for permission to use extracts from the Seafield Muniments.